★ HOCKEY SUPERSTARS ★

STEVEN STAMKOS

BY MATT DOEDEN

CAPSTONE PRESS
a capstone imprint

Sports Illustrated Kids Hockey Superstars published by Capstone Press,
1710 Roe Crest Drive, North Mankato, Minnesota 56003.
www.capstonepub.com

Library of Congress Cataloging-in-Publication Data
Doeden, Matt.
Steven Stamkos / by Matt Doeden.
pages cm. — (Sports Illustrated Kids. Hockey Superstars.)
Includes bibliographical references and index.
Summary: "Details the life and career of hockey superstar Steven Stamkos"— Provided
by publisher.
Audience: Age: 9-15.
Audience: Grade: 4 to 6.
ISBN 978-1-4914-2139-0 (Library Binding)
1. Stamkos, Steven—Juvenile literature. 2. Hockey players—Canada—Biography—
Juvenile literature. I. Title.
GV848.5.S72D64 2015
796.962092—dc23
[B]   2014025987

Editorial Credits
Brenda Haugen, editor; Ted Williams, designer; Eric Gohl, media researcher;
Morgan Walters, production specialist

Photo Credits
Alamy: ZUMA Press, Inc., 23; AP Photo: The Canadian Press/Jesse Johnston, 24–25;
Dreamstime: Jerry Coli, cover, 16, 30–31 (background), 32 (background); Getty Images:
Claus Andersen, 11, NHLI/Gregory Shamus, 1, NHLI/Scott Audette, 14, Toronto Star/
Carlos Osorio, 9 (top), Toronto Star/David Cooper, 27; Newscom: Reuters/Adam Hunger,
20, Reuters/David Denoma, 6, Reuters/Patrick Doyle, 12, UPI/Archie Carpenter, 4;
Sports Illustrated: Damian Strohmeyer, 28–29, David E. Klutho, back cover, 9 (bottom),
18–19, Tony Triolo, 22

Design Elements
Shutterstock

Source Note
Page 7, line 10: "Tampa Bay Lightning Center Steven Stamkos: The Biggest Game of My
Career." Bay News 9. 23 April 2011. 8 July 2014. www.baynews9.com/content/news/
baynews9/news/article.html/content/news/articles/ot/both/2011/04/23/Tampa_Bay_
Lightning_Center_Steven_Stamkos_The_biggest_game_of_my_career.html

Printed in the United States of America in Stevens Point, Wisconsin.
092014   008479WZS15

TABLE OF CONTENTS

CHAPTER 1
BREAKING OUT 5

CHAPTER 2
EARLY LIFE 8

CHAPTER 3
WELCOME TO THE NHL 15

CHAPTER 4
BRIGHT FUTURE 26

GLOSSARY 30

READ MORE 31

INTERNET SITES 31

INDEX..32

CHAPTER 1

BREAKING OUT

The Tampa Bay Lightning were in trouble. They trailed the Pittsburgh Penguins three games to one in the first round of the 2011 National Hockey League (NHL) playoffs. A loss would end the Lightning's season.

Steven Stamkos had been Tampa Bay's biggest star all season. But the 21-year-old **center** hadn't scored a single goal in the first four games of the playoffs. That was about to change.

Late in the first period, Tampa Bay held a 1-0 lead. Stamkos stood near the Pittsburgh goal as **winger** Steve Downie took a shot. Stamkos deflected the shot, and the puck bounced off the Penguins' goaltender. Stamkos reached out for the **rebound** and jammed it into the net. Goal! It was the first playoff goal of Stamkos' career.

center—the player who participates in a face-off at the beginning of play

winger—a type of forward who usually stays near the sides of the zone

rebound—a puck that bounces off the goaltender or the goal

Tampa Bay kept attacking. Early in the second period, Stamkos picked up an assist on a goal by Vincent Lecavalier. A few minutes later, the Lightning were on a **power play**. Stamkos collected a rebound off the Pittsburgh goalie and buried the puck in the back of the net. The Lightning were up 5-0.

The rout was on. Tampa extended its lead to 7-0 and easily held on to win the game 8-2.

"It was the biggest game of my career," Stamkos told reporters after the game. "I've never been in a situation like this and you wanna stay alive in the playoffs. ... I thought I was able to step up to the challenge."

It was the start of something big for Stamkos and the Tampa Bay Lightning. They shocked the Penguins by winning three in a row and stealing the series. Their surprising playoff run took them within a single game of the **Stanley Cup** Finals, due largely to their young superstar.

power play—when a team has a one- or two-player advantage because the other team has one or more players in the penalty box

Stanley Cup—the trophy given each year to the NHL champion

CHAPTER 2

EARLY LIFE

Steven Christopher Stamkos was born February 7, 1990, in Markham, Ontario. Steven grew up in the Toronto suburb with his parents, Chris and Lesley, and his younger sister, Sarah.

Stamkos loved hockey from an early age. He visited local hockey rinks and practiced in his family's dining room. Steven was a gifted athlete and excelled at hockey. He also played lacrosse, golf, baseball, and soccer.

Stamkos combined his rare natural talent with hard work. He spent hours perfecting his shot. He modeled himself after NHL legend Joe Sakic and mastered the **one-timer**.

one-timer—a hard slap shot taken far from the goal

franchise—team

HOCKEY HERO: JOE SAKIC

Joe Sakic was one of Stamkos' favorite players. Sakic spent his entire NHL career with one **franchise**. He started in 1988 with the Quebec Nordiques. They moved to Colorado and became the Avalanche in 1995. Fans loved Sakic's smooth style and rocket-fast wrist shot.

Stamkos played for Brother Andre High School in Markham, Ontario.

Sakic's best season may have been 2000–01. His 54 goals that season ranked second in the NHL. Sakic won the Hart Memorial Trophy as the NHL's most valuable player. He retired in 2009.

Joe Sakic

Stamkos dominated the amateur ranks. In 2005, at age 15, he joined the Markham Waxers of the Ontario Minor Hockey Association. Stamkos was head and shoulders above his competition. In 66 games with the Waxers, he scored 105 goals and added 92 assists. That's an average of almost three points per game!

Then he went on to the Ontario Hockey League (OHL). Stamkos played his next two seasons with the Sarnia Sting. Because he was far from home, Stamkos stayed with a host family, the Shaws. He struck up a friendship with Andrew Shaw, who was a scout for the NHL's Columbus Blue Jackets. But Shaw wasn't the only scout keeping an eye on the teenager. Stamkos was fast becoming one of the hottest NHL prospects in Canada.

FAST FACT

In one game Stamkos and the Waxers trailed 5-1 in the third period. Stamkos scored five goals in the period to give his team an amazing 6-5 victory.

Stamkos and the Sarnia Sting took on the
London Knights in a 2007 game.

Stamkos tried on his Lightning jersey and cap after being drafted in 2008.

Stamkos was already a hockey star, but he never forgot about his schoolwork. He was awarded the Bobby Smith Trophy in 2007. This honor goes to the OHL player who combines great play with academic excellence.

With his intelligence, natural ability, and work ethic, Stamkos was the complete package. The Tampa Bay Lightning selected him with the first pick in the 2008 NHL Entry **Draft**. Stamkos signed a three-year contract with the team.

The Lightning were in a period of change. After a terrible 2007–08 season, they had a new coach, Barry Melrose. During training camp Melrose criticized Stamkos. He questioned whether the 18-year-old was tough enough to play in the NHL. It wasn't what Tampa Bay's front office wanted to hear. Those comments, along with the team's poor start, led the Lightning to fire Melrose just 16 games into the season.

draft—the process of choosing a person to join a sports organization or team

THE TAMPA BAY LIGHTNING

Stamkos has played his whole NHL career with the Tampa Bay Lightning. The Lightning entered the NHL as an expansion team in 1992. Many fans call the team the Bolts, for the lightning bolt logo on their jerseys.

Tampa Bay fans suffered through some tough times early on. The team didn't win a single playoff series until 2003, but that marked the beginning of better days. They won the Stanley Cup in 2004.

CHAPTER 3

WELCOME TO THE NHL

Stamkos' first year had its highs and lows. His first NHL game was in Prague, a city in the Czech Republic. The Lightning lost to the New York Rangers 2-1.

Stamkos didn't score a single point until his eighth game. He tallied his first two goals on October 30 against the Buffalo Sabres.

The personal highlight of Stamkos' **rookie** season came on February 17, 2009, against the Chicago Blackhawks. In the first period, Stamkos streaked down the right side of the ice as Tampa Bay defenseman Josef Melichar took a shot. The shot bounced off Chicago's goaltender. Stamkos grabbed the rebound and slapped it into the net for a goal.

In the second period, Stamkos scored his second goal of the game during a four-minute power play. Less than a minute and a half later, Tampa was still on the power play. Stamkos stood on the left side of the ice. The Lightning cycled the puck around the zone. Defenseman Steve Eminger slid the puck to Stamkos, who drew back his stick and fired a one-timer. Goal! It was his third goal of the game and his first NHL **hat trick**!

rookie—a first-year player

hat trick—when a player scores three goals in one game

After the season, Stamkos joined Team Canada for the 2009 World Championship in Switzerland. Stamkos showed off his talents by scoring seven goals in just nine games. He helped Canada win the silver medal.

Stamkos knew that his game still needed work. He wanted to improve his strength and **endurance**. So he started training with NHL **veteran** Gary Roberts in the off-season.

The extra work paid off. The 19-year-old started the 2009–10 season on fire. He scored 10 goals in Tampa's first 11 games. He kept scoring all season. His 51 goals tied him with Sidney Crosby for the most in the NHL. He was the third-youngest player ever to score 50 or more. Stamkos also led the league in power play goals with 24. But the Lightning struggled as a team. They missed the playoffs again.

endurance—the ability to keep doing an activity for long periods of time

veteran—a longtime player

FAST FACT

Stamkos scored at least one point in 18 straight games starting January 19, 2010.

Stamkos started strong again in 2010–11. Through the first 19 games, he had 19 goals. He scored the 100th goal of his young career December 20, 2010. The league was taking notice. Stamkos was selected to play in the NHL All-Star Game.

Stamkos cooled off in the second half, but the Lightning still finished 46-25-11. That was good enough for a playoff berth, but their opening series started poorly. Tampa trailed

the Penguins 3 games to 1. Then the Lightning shocked
hockey fans by winning their next eight games!

The Lightning faced the Boston Bruins in the Eastern
Conference Finals. It was a hard-fought series. Boston led
3 games to 2. In Game 6 Stamkos scored three points to help
Tampa to a 5-4 victory. It was on to Game 7. The winner
would advance to the Stanley Cup Finals.

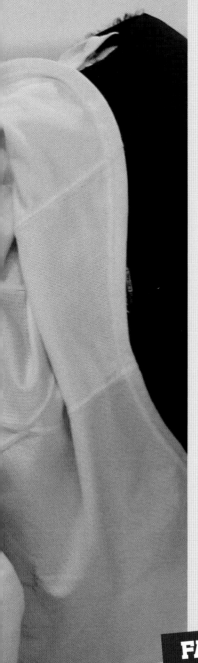

It was a tight, defensive Game 7. The game remained scoreless early in the second period. The Bruins had the puck in the Tampa Bay zone. Boston defenseman Johnny Boychuk fired a hard shot toward the goal. But a Lightning player deflected the shot. Stamkos had no time to react. The puck slammed into his face.

Stamkos fell to the ice. Blood streamed from his nose. He held his face as he skated off the ice.

Stamkos refused to sit out for long. He returned to the game after getting checked out. Any questions about his toughness were answered that night. It wasn't a happy ending for the Lightning, though. The Bruins scored the game's only goal midway through the third period. Tampa Bay's miracle playoff run was over.

FAST FACT

Stamkos didn't miss a single game for four straight seasons. His streak went from 2009–10 to 2012–13.

THE RECORD BOOKS

In 1982 NHL legend Wayne Gretzky set the record for goals in a season with 92. That's an average of more than one goal per game! Many experts believe it's a record that will never be broken.

Wayne Gretzky

Today's NHL is much different than it was 30 years ago. There's a greater focus on defense. Teams understand better how to make scoring difficult for star players. Since 1996 only two NHL players have scored 60 or more goals in a season. They are Alexander Ovechkin (65 in 2007–08) and Stamkos (60 in 2011–12).

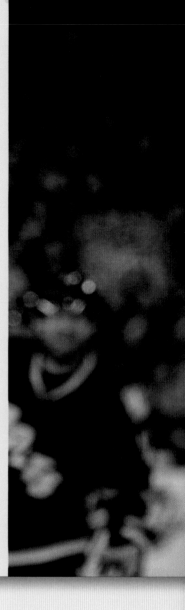

Stamkos and the Lightning agreed to a five-year, $37.5 million contract before the 2011–12 season. Stamkos proved early on that he was worth the big money. He led the NHL with 60 goals. It was the most in Lightning history. He also was an All-Star selection for the second time.

On March 31, 2012, the Lightning and the Winnipeg Jets were tied 2-2 in overtime. From the left side, Stamkos took a pass and fired his famous one-timer. Score! It was his fifth overtime goal of the season, an NHL record.

But it was a disappointing season for the Lightning. Just one year after advancing within a game of the Stanley Cup Finals, they missed the playoffs altogether.

The next two seasons were filled with disappointment for Stamkos and his fans. Players and owners squared off in a dispute before the 2012–13 season. They could not reach an agreement on how the league pays its players. As a result the NHL announced a **lockout**.

Stamkos returned home during the lockout. He enjoyed playing **pickup games** with his dad and friends. The lockout

stretched into 2013 before the two sides came to an agreement. The season didn't start until January 2013. It was a shortened 48-game season. Stamkos finished second in both goals and points. But once again the Lightning struggled and missed the playoffs.

lockout—a period of time in which owners prevent players from reporting to their teams; owners do not pay players during lockouts and no games are played

pickup game—an informal game played for fun

CHAPTER 4

BRIGHT FUTURE

The 2013–14 season started out much brighter for Stamkos and the Lightning. The team had one of the top records in the Eastern Conference when they took the ice against the Bruins November 11, 2013. Stamkos was leading the league in scoring with 14 goals and nine assists.

But in the second period, Stamkos got tied up with a Boston player. Stamkos smashed his leg into the goal post and fell to the ice. He tried to get up but couldn't support his weight. His leg was broken.

It was a crushing blow. Stamkos missed almost four months. The injury also kept him out of the Winter Olympics, where Canada won a gold medal without him.

The Lightning named Stamkos the team captain when he finally returned to the ice on March 6. The team was in the thick of the playoff hunt. Stamkos' return was just what they needed. Just two weeks after coming back from the injury, Stamkos scored a hat trick in a 5-3 victory against the Toronto Maple Leafs. Even more amazing, Stamkos scored his three goals on just three total shots!

The Lightning went on to make the playoffs. Stamkos netted a pair of goals in the opening game against the Montreal Canadiens. But Montreal was just too much for the Lightning, sweeping the Bolts in four games.

Stamkos remains one of the young, up-and-coming stars of the NHL. He may have the most **accurate** shot in the entire league. Opposing defenders always have to know exactly where he is on the ice.

Stamkos was a key part of the 2011 Lightning team that went all the way to the Eastern Conference Finals. But 2014 was his only other trip to the playoffs, and the Lightning

were swept in their opening series. Can Stamkos help the team turn things around?

One thing seems sure. As long as he stays healthy, Stamkos will remain one of the most dangerous scorers in the game. And his fans will never get tired of watching him unleash his signature one-timer.

accurate—on target

GLOSSARY

accurate (AK-yuh-ruht)—on target

center (SEN-tur)—the player who participates in a face-off at the beginning of play

draft (DRAFT)—the process of choosing a person to join a sports organization or team

endurance (en-DUR-enss)—the ability to keep doing an activity for long periods of time

franchise (FRAN-chize)—team

hat trick (HAT TRIK)—when a player scores three goals in one game

lockout (LOK-out)—a period of time in which owners prevent players from reporting to their teams; owners do not pay players during lockouts and no games are played

one-timer (WUHN TYE-mur)—a hard slap shot taken far from the goal

pickup game (PIK-uhp GAYM)—an informal game played for fun

power play (POW-ur PLAY)—when a team has a one- or two-player advantage because the other team has one or more players in the penalty box

rebound (REE-bound)—a puck that bounces off the goaltender or the goal

rookie (RUK-ee)—a first-year player

Stanley Cup (STAN-lee KUP)—the trophy given each year to the NHL champion

veteran (VET-ur-uhn)—a longtime player

winger (WING-ur)—a type of forward who usually stays near the sides of the zone

READ MORE

Doeden, Matt. *Sidney Crosby: Hockey Superstar.* Superstar Athletes. North Mankato, Minn.: Capstone Press, 2012.

Frederick, Shane. *The Ultimate Guide to Pro Hockey Teams.* Ultimate Pro Team Guides. North Mankato, Minn.: Capstone Press, 2011.

Gitlin, Marty. *Hockey.* Minneapolis: ABDO Pub., 2012.

INTERNET SITES

FactHound offers a safe, fun way to find Internet sites related to this book. All of the sites on FactHound have been researched by our staff.

Here's all you do:

Visit *www.facthound.com*

Type in this code: 9781491421390

Check out projects, games and lots more at
www.capstonekids.com

INDEX

Bobby Smith Trophy, 13
Boston Bruins, 19, 21, 26
Boychuk, Johnny, 21
Buffalo Sabres, 15

Chicago Blackhawks, 15
Colorado Avalanche, 8
Columbus Blue Jackets, 10
Crosby, Sidney, 17
Czech Republic, 15

Downie, Steve, 5

Eminger, Steve, 15

Gretzky, Wayne, 22

Hart Memorial Trophy, 9

Lecavalier, Vincent, 7

Markham Waxers, 10
Melichar, Josef, 15
Melrose, Barry, 13
Montreal Canadiens, 26

National Hockey League
    (NHL)
    All-Star Game, 18, 22
    draft, 13
    lockout, 24–25
New York Rangers, 15

Ovechkin, Alexander, 22

Pittsburgh Penguins, 5, 7,
    18–19

Quebec Nordiques, 8

Roberts, Gary, 17

Sakic, Joe, 8–9
Sarnia Sting, 10
Shaw, Andrew, 10
Stamkos, Steven
    birth, 8
    family, 8
    first NHL goal, 15
    first NHL hat trick, 15
    first NHL playoff goal, 5
    growing up, 8
    host family, 10
    injuries, 21, 26
    named team captain, 26
    NHL contract, 22
    on video game cover, 23

Stanley Cup, 7, 13, 19, 23

Tampa Bay Lightning, 5, 7,
    13, 15, 17, 18, 19, 21, 22,
    23, 25, 26, 28–29
Team Canada, 17, 26
Toronto Maple Leafs, 26

Winnipeg Jets, 23